Collins

真正上海数学

# Real Shanghai Mathematics

## Practice Book

**2.1**

世纪出版

少年兒童出版社
Juvenile & Children's Publishing House

**MIX**
Paper from
responsible sources
FSC™ C007454

This book is produced from independently certified FSC paper
to ensure responsible forest management.

For more information visit: **www.harpercollins.co.uk/green**

William Collins' dream of knowledge for all began with the publication of his first book in 1819. A self-educated mill worker, he not only enriched millions of lives, but also founded a flourishing publishing house. Today, staying true to this spirit, Collins books are packed with inspiration, innovation and practical expertise. They place you at the centre of a world of possibility and give you exactly what you need to explore it.

Collins. Freedom to teach.

**Collins**
An imprint of HarperCollins*Publishers*
The News Building
1 London Bridge Street
London
SE1 9GF

**Browse the complete Collins catalogue at**
**www.collins.co.uk**

© Shanghai Schools (Pre-Schools) Curriculum Reform
  Commission 2007
© Shanghai Century Publishing Group Co., Ltd. 2018
© HarperCollinsPublishers Limited 2018

Published by arrangement with Shanghai Century Publishing
Group Co., Ltd.

10 9 8 7 6 5 4 3

ISBN 978-0-00-826164-1

The educational materials in this book were compiled in accordance with the course curriculum produced by the Shanghai Schools (Pre-Schools) Curriculum Reform Commission and 'Maths Syllabus for Shanghai Schools (Trial Implementation)' for use in Primary 2 First Term under the nine-year compulsory education system.

These educational materials were compiled by the head of Shanghai Normal University, and reviewed and approved for trial use by Shanghai Schools Educational Materials Review Board.

The writers for this book's educational materials are:
Editor-in-Chief: Huang Jianhong
Guest Writers: Huang Jianhong, Tong Hui, Xu Peijing, Chen Peiqun, Zheng Kaida, Chen Chungen, Yan Xiaohong, Song Yongfu

This volume's "Practice Book" was revised by:
"Primary School Maths Practice Book" Compilation Team

British Library Cataloguing in Publication Data
A catalogue record for this publication is available from the British Library.

For the English edition:

Primary Publishing Director: Lee Newman
Primary Publishing Managers: Fiona McGlade, Lizzie Catford
Editorial Project Manager: Mike Appleton
Editorial Manager: Amanda Harman
Editorial Assistant: Holly Blood
Managing Translator: Huang Xingfeng
Translators: Bian Xinyuan, Huang Chunhua, Shi Jiamin, Wang Yinan, Yang Lili, Ye Huini
Lead Editor: Tanya Solomons
Copyeditor: Denise Moulton
Proofreader: Denise Moulton, Life Lines Editorial Services, Helen Bleck, Joan Miller
Cover artist: Amparo Barrera
Designer: Ken Vail Graphic Design
Production Controller: Sarah Burke
Printed and bound by CPI Group (UK) Ltd, Croydon, CR0 4YY

**Photo acknowledgements**
The publishers wish to thank the following for permission to reproduce photographs. Every effort has been made to trace copyright holders and to obtain their permission for the use of copyright materials. The publishers will gladly receive any information enabling them to rectify any error or omission at the first opportunity.

(t = top, c = centre, b = bottom, r = right, l = left)

p3tl Reamolko/Shutterstock, p3tc Reamolko/Shutterstock, p3tr Reamolko/Shutterstock, p3bl Giraffarte/Shutterstock, p3br Reamolko/Shutterstock, p46 wavebreakmedia/Shutterstock, p74 Reinhold Leitner/Shutterstock

All other images with permission from Shanghai Century Publishing Group.

# Contents

# Unit One: Revising and improving

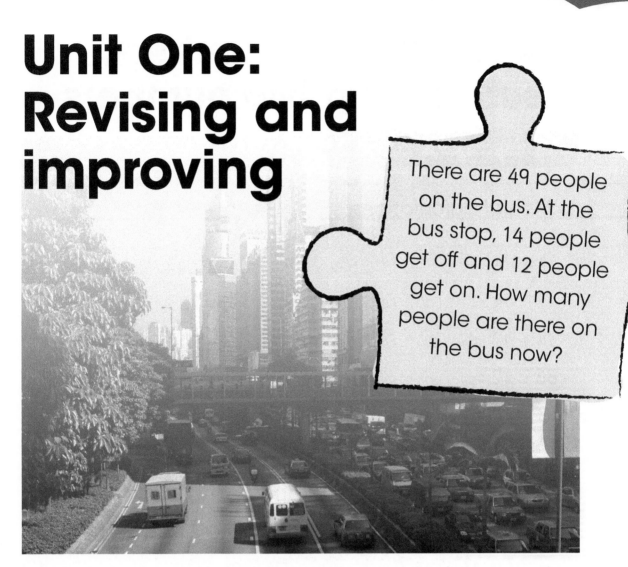

There are 49 people on the bus. At the bus stop, 14 people get off and 12 people get on. How many people are there on the bus now?

The table below lists the sections in this unit.
After completing each section, assess your work.
(Use 😊 if you are satisfied with your progress or 😕 if you are not satisfied.)

| Section | Self-assessment |
| --- | --- |
| 1. Adding three numbers, subtracting two numbers | |
| 2. Addition and subtraction | |
| 3. Intelligent practice | |
| 4. Fill in the missing numbers | |

# 1. Adding three numbers, subtracting two numbers

**Pupil Textbook page 2**

Level **A**

## 1. Mental calculations

| | | |
|---|---|---|
| 69 – 6 = | 36 + 7 = | 44 – 5 = |
| 77 – 9 = | 76 + 8 = | 23 + 25 = |
| 34 + 43 = | 55 – 13 = | 25 + 10 = |
| 86 – 12 = | 38 + 59 = | 62 – 17 = |
| 33 + 18 = | 43 + 38 = | 43 – 38 = |

## 2. Use quick calculation methods and write the answers.

a. 24 + 16 + 37 =          54 + 26 + 15 =

   46 + 17 + 24 =

b. 45 – 15 – 22 =          77 – 24 – 16 =

   54 – 27 – 27 =

c. 72 – 38 + 38 =          25 + 38 – 34 =

   61 – 22 + 28 =

## 3. Apply.

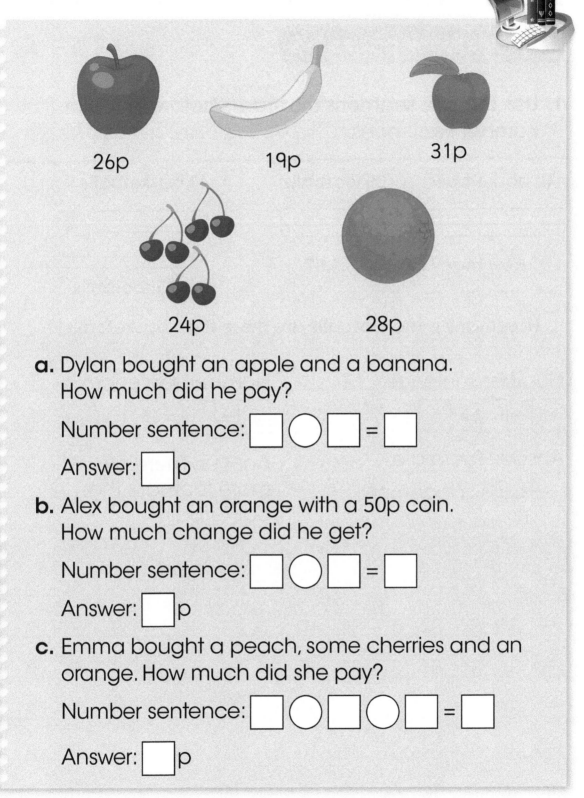

26p

19p

31p

24p

28p

**a.** Dylan bought an apple and a banana.
How much did he pay?

Number sentence: ☐ ◯ ☐ = ☐

Answer: ☐p

**b.** Alex bought an orange with a 50p coin.
How much change did he get?

Number sentence: ☐ ◯ ☐ = ☐

Answer: ☐p

**c.** Emma bought a peach, some cherries and an
orange. How much did she pay?

Number sentence: ☐ ◯ ☐ ◯ ☐ = ☐

Answer: ☐p

# 2. Addition and subtraction

**Pupil Textbook pages 3–5**

**1.** Use the line segment diagrams below to make number sentences.

40 basketballs        55 footballs

**How many balls in total?**

40 basketballs

55 footballs

**How many more footballs are there than basketballs?**

Number sentence:

☐ + ☐ = ☐

Answer: There are
☐ balls altogether.

Number sentence:

☐ – ☐ = ☐

Answer: There are ☐
more footballs than
basketballs.

## 2. Complete the line segment diagrams and write number sentences.

There are 16 ducks on the bank and 25 ducks on the lake.

**a.** How many ducks are there altogether?

| 16 ducks | |
|---|---|

Number sentence:

☐ ◯ ☐ = ☐

Answer:

There are ☐ ducks altogether.

**b.** How many fewer ducks are on the bank than on the lake?

Number sentence:

☐ ◯ ☐ = ☐

Answer:

There are ☐ fewer ducks on the bank than on the lake.

**3.** Use the line segment diagram below to make a number sentence. Talk about the meaning of the question first.

How much has Alex
spent, in pence?          Alex has 32p left.

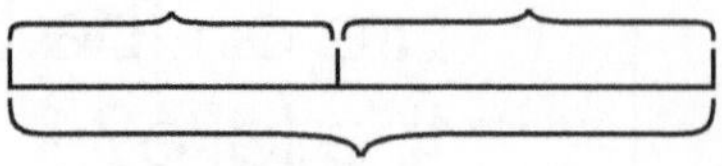

He had **60p** to start with.

Number sentence:

□ ◯ □ = □

Answer:
Alex has spent ☐ p

Level **B**

## Ask some relevant questions and then answer them.

A football is made from 12 pieces of black leather and 20 pieces of white leather.

Question 1: _____

Number sentence: _____

Answer: _____

Question 2: _____

Number sentence: _____

Answer: _____

# 3. Intelligent practice

Pupil Textbook pages 6-7

Level **A**

**1.** Find the rule and fill in the missing numbers.

a.
$$49 + 6 = 50 + \boxed{\phantom{0}}$$
$$47 + 6 = 50 + \boxed{\phantom{0}}$$

b.
$$15 + 79 = \boxed{\phantom{0}} + 80$$
$$15 + 77 = \boxed{\phantom{0}} + 80$$

c.
$$81 - 9 = \boxed{\phantom{0}} - 10$$
$$81 - 7 = \boxed{\phantom{0}} - 10$$

d.
$$43 - 39 = \boxed{\phantom{0}} - 40$$
$$43 - 37 = \boxed{\phantom{0}} - 40$$

**2.** Calculate using the most efficient method.

$$39 + 7 = 40 + \boxed{\phantom{0}} = \boxed{\phantom{0}}$$
$$82 - 8 = \boxed{\phantom{0}} - 10 = \boxed{\phantom{0}}$$
$$26 + 47 = \boxed{\phantom{0}} + 50 = \boxed{\phantom{0}}$$
$$39 - 12 = \boxed{\phantom{0}} - 10 = \boxed{\phantom{0}}$$

$$68 + 14 = \boxed{\phantom{0}} + \boxed{\phantom{0}} = \boxed{\phantom{0}}$$
$$97 - 79 = \boxed{\phantom{0}} - \boxed{\phantom{0}} = \boxed{\phantom{0}}$$
$$35 + 59 = \boxed{\phantom{0}} + \boxed{\phantom{0}} = \boxed{\phantom{0}}$$
$$76 - 33 = \boxed{\phantom{0}} - \boxed{\phantom{0}} = \boxed{\phantom{0}}$$

Level **B**

Calculate using your preferred method.

a.
$$55 + 27 = \boxed{\phantom{0}}$$
$$55 - 27 = \boxed{\phantom{0}}$$

b.
$$43 + 19 = \boxed{\phantom{0}}$$
$$43 - 19 = \boxed{\phantom{0}}$$

# 4. Fill in the missing numbers

Level **A**

**1.** Use the line segment diagrams below to make number sentences.

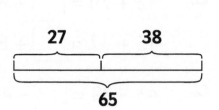

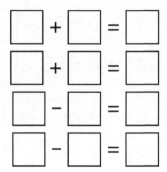

**2.** Use the line segment diagrams to help you fill in the missing numbers.

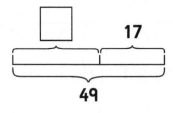

$32 + \boxed{\phantom{0}} = 49$

Think: $49 - 32 = \boxed{\phantom{0}}$

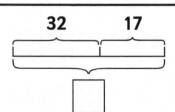

$49 - \boxed{\phantom{0}} = 17$

Think: $49 \bigcirc 17 = \boxed{\phantom{0}}$

$\boxed{\phantom{0}} - 32 = 17$

Think: $\boxed{\phantom{0}} \bigcirc \boxed{\phantom{0}} = \boxed{\phantom{0}}$

**3.** Complete the number sentences.

**a.**

21 + ☐ = 45      72 − ☐ = 51      ☐ − 6 = 25

☐ + 9 = 20      57 − ☐ = 33      ☐ − 11 = 25

**b.**

54 + ☐ = 66      ☐ + 14 = 29      ☐ − 32 = 29

66 − ☐ = 54      ☐ − 14 = 29      32 − ☐ = 29

Level **B**

When the bus arrives at a bus stop **8** people get off the bus and **8** people get on. Now there are **43** people on the bus. How many people were there on the bus originally?

9

# Unit Two: Multiplication and division (1)

> How many times greater is the number of giraffes than the number of zebras?

The table below lists the sections in this unit.
After completing each section, assess your work.
(Draw 😊 if you are satisfied with your progress or 😐 if you are not satisfied.)

| Section | |
|---|---|
| 1. Introduction to multiplication | |
| 2. Look at the picture and write the multiplication sentences | |
| 3. Times | |
| 4. Multiplication of 10 | |
| 5. Multiplication of 5 | |
| 6. Multiplication of 2 | |
| 7. Multiplication of 4 | |

| Section | |
|---|---|
| 8. Multiplication of 8 | |
| 9. Relationships between multiplications of 2, 4 and 8 | |
| 10. Dividing and division | |
| 11. Using times tables to find the quotient | |
| 12. How many times? | |
| 13. Division with the dividend 0 | |

# 1. Introduction to multiplication

1. Use the pictures to help you fill in the missing numbers.

   a.

   $\boxed{\phantom{0}} + \boxed{\phantom{0}} + \boxed{\phantom{0}} = \boxed{\phantom{0}}$        $\boxed{\phantom{0}}$ ____ s

   added together is $\boxed{\phantom{0}}$.

   b.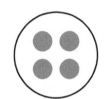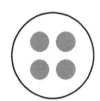

   $\boxed{\phantom{0}}$ ____ s        $\boxed{\phantom{0}} + \boxed{\phantom{0}} + \boxed{\phantom{0}} = \boxed{\phantom{0}}$

2. Circle the dots and complete the sentences.

   a.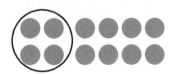

   ____ fours added together is $\boxed{\phantom{0}}$.

   Addition sentence: _____

b.

4 fives added together is ☐.
Addition sentence:

_____

─────────────────────────────────────── **Level B**

## Circle the triangles in two ways. Then complete the sentences.

a.

☐____s added together is ☐.
Addition sentence:

_____

b.

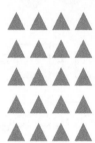

☐____s added together is ☐.
Addition sentence:

_____

**1.** **Use the pictures to help you answer the questions.**

**a.** How many pears are there?

☐ ____s added together

Addition sentence: ☐ + ☐ + ☐ + ☐ = ☐ (pears)

Multiplication sentence: ☐ × ☐ = ☐ (pears)

**b.** How many cherries are there?

There are ☐ cherries 🍒 in each bunch.

There are ☐ bunches.

There are ☐ cherries 🍒 altogether.

☐ ____s added together

Addition sentence: _____ = ☐ (cherries)

Multiplication sentence:

_____ = ☐ (cherries)

The factors are ☐ and ☐. The product is ☐.

The multiplication sentence reads: _____.

## 2. From addition sentences to multiplication sentences

3 + 3 + 3 + 3 + 3 = 15

□ × □ = □

4 + 4 + 4 + 4 + 4 + 4 = □

□ × □ = □

2 + 2 + 2 + 2 + 2 + 2 + 2 + 2 + 2 + 2 = □

□ × □ = □

5 + 5 + 5 = 15

□ × □ = □

8 + 8 + 8 = □

□ × □ = □

10 + 10 + 10 + 10 = □

□ × □ = □

Level **B**

## Circle and complete.

a.

□____s added together

There are □ footballs altogether.

Addition sentence:

_____

Multiplication sentence:

_____

b.

□____s added together

There are □ model planes altogether.

Addition sentence:

_____

Multiplication sentence:

_____

**1.** Use the pictures to help you fill in the missing numbers.

**a.**

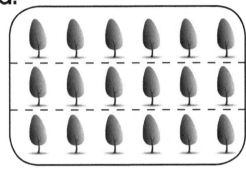

☐ _____s added together    ☐ _____s added together

☐ × ☐ = ☐    ☐ × ☐ = ☐

☐ × ☐ = ☐ × ☐

**b.**

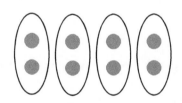        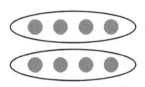

☐ _____s added    ☐ _____s added

together is ☐.    together is ☐.

Addition sentence:    Addition sentence:

_____    _____

Multiplication sentence:    Multiplication sentence:

_____    _____

☐ × ☐ = ☐ × ☐

**2.** Fill in the missing numbers.

a. $3 \times 7 = \boxed{\phantom{0}} + \boxed{\phantom{0}} + \boxed{\phantom{0}} = \boxed{\phantom{0}}$

$7 \times 3 = \boxed{\phantom{0}} + \boxed{\phantom{0}} + \boxed{\phantom{0}} + \boxed{\phantom{0}} + \boxed{\phantom{0}} + \boxed{\phantom{0}} + \boxed{\phantom{0}} = \boxed{\phantom{0}}$

$$\boxed{\phantom{0}} \times \boxed{\phantom{0}} = \boxed{\phantom{0}} \times \boxed{\phantom{0}}$$

b. $3 \times 5 = 5 \times \boxed{\phantom{0}}$ $\qquad$ $8 \times 6 = \boxed{\phantom{0}} \times \boxed{\phantom{0}}$

$4 \times 7 = \boxed{\phantom{0}} \times 4$ $\qquad$ $2 \times 9 = \boxed{\phantom{0}} \times \boxed{\phantom{0}}$

**3.** Make the operation simple by exchanging the positions of the factors.

$6 \times 2 = 2 \times 6 = \boxed{\phantom{0}} + \boxed{\phantom{0}} = \boxed{\phantom{0}}$

$3 + 3 + 3 + 3 + 3 = \boxed{\phantom{0}} \times \boxed{\phantom{0}} = \boxed{\phantom{0}} \times \boxed{\phantom{0}} = \boxed{\phantom{0}}$

Level **B**

Think about the problem, work out the answer and then fill in the missing numbers.

a. ■ + ■ = 10

■ = ( )

b. ■ + ■ + ■ + ■ + ■ = 10

■ = ( )

c. ▲ + ▲ + ▲ = 18

▲ = ( )

d. ▲ + ▲ = 18

▲ = ( )

# 2. Look at the picture and write the multiplication sentences

**Pupil Textbook pages 16–17**

1. Complete the multiplication sentences, using the pictures to help you.

a.

There are ( ) rows of watermelons and there are ( ) watermelons in each row.

There are ( ) columns of watermelons and there are ( ) watermelons in each column.

_____

b.

_____

_____

_____

_____

**1. Look at the picture and make up some sentences about it.**

There are ☐ books in each group and there are ☐ groups altogether.

Question: _____

Sentence: _____

Answer: _____

**2. Draw a different array with 12 dots. Then write the multiplication sentence on the line.**

For example:  12 = 3 × 4 = 4 × 3        _____

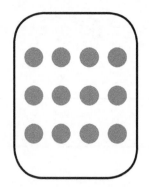

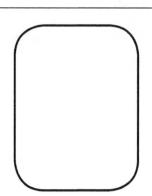

# 3. Times

Pupil Textbook pages 18–21

Level A

1. Fill in the missing numbers, using the pictures to help you.

a.

  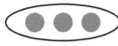 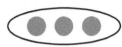

If 3 ▲ is 1 part, the number of ● is ( ) parts.

The number of ● is ( ) times the number of ▲, which is ( ) times ( ).

Number sentence: ☐ × ☐ = ☐

b.

 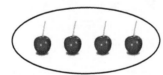 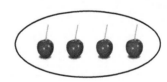

If 4 🍓 is 1 part, the number of 🍒 is ( ) parts.

The number of 🍒 is ( ) times the number of 🍓, which is ( ) times ( ).

Number sentence: ☐ × ☐ = ☐

## 2. Circle and complete.

If 2 bear biscuits is 1 part, the number of rabbit biscuits is ( ) parts.

The number of ( ) biscuits is ( ) times the number of ( ) biscuits, which is ( ) times ( ).

Number sentence: ☐ × ☐ = ☐

## 3. Fill in the missing numbers.

2 + 2 + 2 + 2 + 2 + 2 = ☐

☐ twos added together

☐ times 2

6 × 2 = ☐

2 × 6 = ☐

8 + 8 + 8 + 8 = ☐

☐☐ s added together

☐ times ☐

☐ × ☐ = ☐

☐ × ☐ = ☐

9 + 9 + 9 = ☐

☐☐ s added together

☐ times ☐

☐ × ☐ = ☐

☐ × ☐ = ☐

**4.** Draw lines to match the pairs.

| | |
|---|---|
| 6 + 6 + 6 + 6 | 3 times 5 |
| 5 + 5 + 5 | 4 times 2 |
| 2 + 2 + 2 + 2 | 4 times 6 |
| 4 + 4 + 4 + 4 + 4 + 4 | 6 times 4 |

Level **B**

**1.** Circle the shapes. Then work out the answer and write the number sentence.

**a.** The number of ■ is 2 times the number of ●.
● ● ● ●

_____

Number sentence:

_____

**b.** The number of ▲ is 3 times the number of .
★ ★ ★

_____

Number sentence:

_____

**2.** Draw the missing pictures. The number of ◎ on the right is 2 times the number of  on the left.

| | |
|---|---|
| ● ● ● ● ● | |
| | ◎ ◎ ◎ ◎ |

# 4. Multiplication of 10

**Pupil Textbook pages 22-23**

Level **A**

## 1. Complete the sequences.

a. 10, 20, 30, 40, ____, ____, ____, ____, ____, ____

b. 100, 90, 80, 70, ____, ____, ____, ____, ____, ____

c. 0, ____, 40, ____, 80, ____

## 2. Fill in the missing numbers.

$$10 \times \begin{array}{|c|} \hline 1 \\ \hline 3 \\ \hline 5 \\ \hline 7 \\ \hline 9 \\ \hline \end{array} = \begin{array}{|c|} \hline \\ \hline \\ \hline \\ \hline \\ \hline \\ \hline \end{array} \qquad \begin{array}{|c|} \hline 0 \\ \hline 2 \\ \hline \\ \hline 8 \\ \hline \\ \hline \end{array} \times 10 = \begin{array}{|c|} \hline \\ \hline \\ \hline 40 \\ \hline \\ \hline 100 \\ \hline \end{array}$$

## 3. Fill in the missing numbers.

$1 \times 10 = \boxed{\phantom{0}}$          $5 \times 10 = \boxed{\phantom{0}}$          $6 \times 10 + 8 = \boxed{\phantom{0}}$

$7 \times 10 = \boxed{\phantom{0}}$          $10 \times 10 = \boxed{\phantom{0}}$          $8 \times 10 - 6 = \boxed{\phantom{0}}$

$10 \times 0 = \boxed{\phantom{0}}$          $10 \times 4 = \boxed{\phantom{0}}$          $10 - 0 \times 10 = \boxed{\phantom{0}}$

$10 \times 2 = \boxed{\phantom{0}}$          $10 \times 9 = \boxed{\phantom{0}}$          $4 + 2 \times 10 = \boxed{\phantom{0}}$

$30 = \boxed{\phantom{0}} \times 10$          $80 = 10 \times \boxed{\phantom{0}}$

**4.** Read each question carefully and work out the answer.

   **a.** There are 10 biscuits on each plate.
      How many biscuits are there on 4 plates?

   ☐ × ☐ = ☐      Answer: There are ☐ biscuits
                                        altogether.

   **b.** Poppy has 10 pencils. Emma has 5 times as many
      as Poppy. How many pencils does Emma have?

   ☐ × ☐ = ☐      Answer: Emma has ☐ pencils.

Level **B**

   **a.** There are 10 balloons in a row.
      How many balloons are in 3 rows?

      Number sentence: ☐ × ☐ = ☐

      Answer: There are ☐ balloons altogether.

   **b.** How many small balloons
      are there altogether?

      Number sentence:

      _____

      Answer: There are ☐
      small balloons altogether.

# 5. Multiplication of 5

**Pupil Textbook pages 24–26**

**1.** Complete the sequence.

5, 10, 15, 20, ____, ____, ____, ____, ____, ____

**2.** Use times tables and write the answers in the brackets.

3 times 5 is ( ).　　　　　5 times 9 is ( ).

1 times 5 is ( ).　　　　　( ) times 6 is 30.

5 times ( ) is 35.　　　　　( ) times 5 is 25.

5 times ( ) is 40.　　　　　2 times ( ) is 10.

( ) times 5 is 20.

**3.** Fill in the missing numbers.

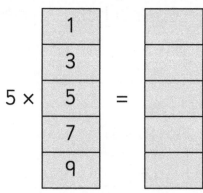

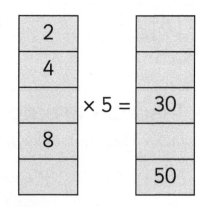

**4.** Reason, calculate and complete.

$3 \times 5 = 15$　　　　　　　　　$10 \times 5 = 50$

$4 \times 5 = 15 + 5 = ($　　$)$　　　$9 \times 5 = 50 - 5 = ($　　$)$

$5 \times 5 = ($　　$) + 5 = ($　　$)$　　$8 \times 5 = ($　　$) - 5 = ($　　$)$

$6 \times 5 = ($　　$) + ($　　$) = ($　　$)$

$7 \times 5 = ($　　$) - ($　　$) = ($　　$)$

**5. Read each question carefully and work out the answer.**

a. There are 5 watermelons in each pile.
How many watermelons are there in 4 piles?

□ × □ = □

Answer: There are □
watermelons altogether.

b. There are 7 black swans at the zoo. The number of white swans is 5 times the number of black swans. How many white swans are there?
How many white swans and black swans are there altogether?

□ ○ □ = □          □ ○ □ = □

Answer:
There are □ white
swans.

Answer:
There are □ white
swans and black
swans altogether.

Level **B**

**Complete.**

I have 5 ★.

My number of ★ is 4 times Alex's.

**Alex**

My number of ★ is twice Alex's.

**Poppy**

**Emma**        Emma has □ ★. Poppy has □ ★.

# 6. Multiplication of 2

**Pupil Textbook pages 27–28**

**1.** Complete the sequence.

2, 4, ____, 8, ____, ____, 14, ____, ____, 20

**2.** Use times tables and write the answers in the brackets.

2 times 9 is (   ).

1 times (   ) is 2.

2 times 5 is (   ).

2 times 2 is (   ).

2 times (   ) is 8.

(   ) times 3 is 6.

2 times 8 is (   ).

2 times (   ) is 14.

(   ) is 6 times 2.

**3.** Fill in the missing numbers.

| Factor | 2 | 3 | 0 | 10 | 2 |
|---|---|---|---|---|---|
| Factor | 4 | | 2 | 2 | 5 |
| Product | | 6 | | | |

**4.** Work out the answers.

**a.** What is 2 times 5?

**b.** Two factors are both 2. What is the product?

**c.** What is the result of adding 2 six times?

**d.** What is the sum of 6 and 2?

**5.** Read each question carefully and work out the answer.

> **a.** There are 8 chocolates in each box.
> How many chocolates are there in 2 boxes?
>
> **b.**
>
>
>
>
>
> There are ☐ hens. The number of cockerels is ☐ times the number of hens. So there are ☐ cockerels.

Level **B**

**1.** A rubber  costs £2. Alex has £15. Is it enough to buy 7 rubbers  ?

**2.** Work out the answers and write the missing numbers in the brackets.

If ● + ● + ● + ● = 8 and ★ + ● + ● = 13,

then ● = (      ), ★ = (      ), ★ × ● = (      ).

# 7. Multiplication of 4

Pupil Textbook pages 29–30

Level **A**

**1. Complete the sequence.**

4, 8, 12, 16, _____, _____, _____, _____, _____, _____

**2. First use times tables and write the answers in the brackets. Then write two multiplication sentences for each one.**

( ) times 9 is 36.                    4 times ( ) is 20.

_____        _____

_____        _____

2 times ( ) is 8.

_____

_____

**3. Fill in the missing numbers.**

$4 \times 0 = \square$     $2 \times 4 = \square$     $4 \times 5 = \square$     $4 \times 3 = \square$

$4 \times 9 = \square$     $10 \times 4 = \square$     $8 \times 4 = \square$     $7 \times 4 = \square$

$4 \times 6 = \square$     $1 \times 4 = \square$

**4. Fill in the missing numbers.**

**a.** 2 fours added is ( ).
2 fours multiplied is ( ).

**b.** $4 + 4 + 4 = ($ $) \times ($ $)$
There are ( ) groups of ( ),
which is ( ) times ( ).

**5.** Read each question carefully and work out the answer.

a. There are 4 legs on each chair.
How many legs are there on 6 chairs?

Number sentence: _____

Answer: _____

b. There are 4 people in each small boat. There are three times as many people in a big boat as in a small boat. How many people are there in a big boat?

The number sentence is: _____

Answer: _____

Level **B**

**1.** There are 4 quarters in a year.
How many quarters are there in 7 years?

**2.** A llama and 4 alpacas are in a field. How many animals are there altogether in the field?
How many feet are there altogether?

# 8. Multiplication of 8

**Pupil Textbook pages 31–33**

Level **A**

**1.** Complete the sequence.

8, 16, _____, 32, _____, _____, 56, 64, _____, _____

**2.** Fill in the missing numbers.

$10 \times 8 = \boxed{\phantom{0}}$  $4 \times 8 = \boxed{\phantom{0}}$  $8 \times 5 - 5 = \boxed{\phantom{0}}$

$8 \times 7 = \boxed{\phantom{0}}$  $8 \times 0 = \boxed{\phantom{0}}$  $9 \times 8 + 5 = \boxed{\phantom{0}}$

$5 \times 8 = \boxed{\phantom{0}}$  $56 = \boxed{\phantom{0}} \times 8$  $6 + 8 \times 3 = \boxed{\phantom{0}}$

$72 = 8 \times \boxed{\phantom{0}}$  $81 - 8 \times 5 = \boxed{\phantom{0}}$

**3.** Read each question carefully and work out the answer.

**a.** Poppy is 8 years old.
Her mother's age is 4 times Poppy's age.
How old is her mother?

**b.** Alex borrowed a storybook. He finished reading the book by reading 8 pages every day for a week. How many pages were in his book?

**c.** There are 2 groups of 8 swans in the lake. How many swans are there altogether?

Level **B**

**1.** There are 8 red fish in the fish bowl. The number of black fish is the same as the number of red fish. How many fish are there altogether?

**2.** Simple calculation

1 + 3 + 1 + 3 + 1 + 3 + 1 + 3 + 1 + 3 + 1 + 3 + 1 + 3 + 1 + 3

= (  ) × (  )

= (  )

# 9. Relationships between multiplications of 2, 4 and 8

**Pupil Textbook pages 34–35**

Level **A**

**1.** Complete the table.

| × | 2 | 4 | 6 | 8 | 1 | 3 | 5 | 7 | 9 |
|---|---|---|---|---|---|---|---|---|---|
| 2 |   |   |   |   |   |   |   |   |   |
| 4 |   |   |   |   |   |   |   |   |   |
| 8 |   |   |   |   |   |   |   |   |   |

**2.** Fill in the missing numbers.

$4 = \boxed{\phantom{0}} \times 4$       $8 = \boxed{\phantom{0}} \times 8$       $12 = \boxed{\phantom{0}} \times 4$       $16 = \boxed{\phantom{0}} \times 8$

$4 = \boxed{\phantom{0}} \times 2$       $8 = \boxed{\phantom{0}} \times 4$       $12 = \boxed{\phantom{0}} \times 2$       $16 = \boxed{\phantom{0}} \times 4$

$8 = \boxed{\phantom{0}} \times 2$       $16 = \boxed{\phantom{0}} \times 2$

What do you notice?

Complete the number sentences below.

$1 \times 4 = \boxed{\phantom{0}} \times 2$       $3 \times 4 = \boxed{\phantom{0}} \times 2$       $1 \times 8 = \boxed{\phantom{0}} \times 4$

$2 \times 8 = \boxed{\phantom{0}} \times 4$       $5 \times 8 = \boxed{\phantom{0}} \times 4$       $1 \times 8 = \boxed{\phantom{0}} \times 2$

**3.** Mental calculations

$3 \times 2 =$       $6 \times 2 =$       $9 \times 2 =$

$3 \times 4 =$       $6 \times 4 =$       $4 \times 9 =$

$3 \times 8 =$       $6 \times 8 =$       $8 \times 9 =$

What do you notice?

**4.** Use the diagram to help you complete the number sentence.

| 2 | 2 | 2 | 2 |
|---|---|---|---|
| 4 | | 4 | |
| 8 | | | |

☐ × ☐ = ☐ × ☐ = ☐ × ☐ = ☐

Level **B**

**1.** There are 4 buses. The number of cars is twice the number of buses.

**a.** How many cars are there?

**b.** How many car wheels are there?

**2.** If the Year 2 Class 2 pupils are divided into 3 groups, each group will have 8 pupils. If each group has 4 pupils, how many groups can the class be divided into? (Remember: Think, complete and calculate.)

☐ × ☐ = ( ) × ☐

# 10. Dividing and division

**Pupil Textbook pages 36–37**

1. **Fill in the missing numbers, using the pictures to help you.**

   **a.** There are 6 tulips in a bunch. How many bunches can you make with 18 tulips?

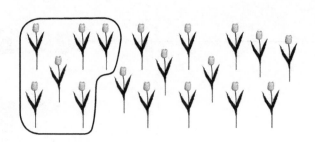

   $18 - 6 - 6 - \boxed{\phantom{0}} = 0$

   (   ) groups of 6

   There are (   ) groups of 6 in 18.

   $18 = ( \phantom{0} ) \times ( \phantom{0} )$

   **b.**

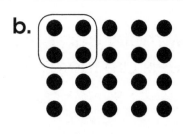

   $20 - \boxed{\phantom{0}} - \boxed{\phantom{0}} - \boxed{\phantom{0}} - \boxed{\phantom{0}} - \boxed{\phantom{0}} = 0$

   (   ) groups of 4

   There are (   ) groups of 4 in 20.

   $20 = ( \phantom{0} ) \times ( \phantom{0} )$

   **c.** Each jump is 8 units on the number line. How many jumps are needed to reach 24?

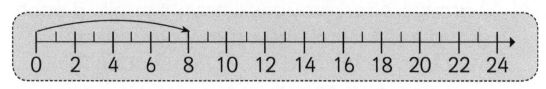

   Jump (   ) times.

   There are (   ) groups of 8 in 24.

   $24 = ( \phantom{0} ) \times ( \phantom{0} )$

**2.** Circle the shapes and fill in the missing numbers.

a.
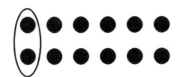
There are ( ) groups of 2 in 12.

12 = ( ) × 2

b.

There are ( ) groups of
( ) in ( ).
( ) = ( ) × ( )

Look at the picture. Count, circle and fill in the missing numbers.

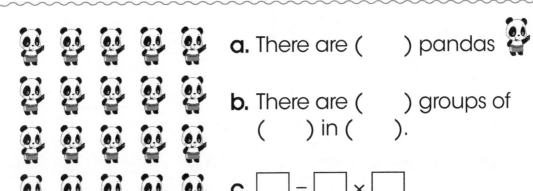

a. There are ( ) pandas .

b. There are ( ) groups of
( ) in ( ).

c. ▢ = ▢ × ▢

**Pupil Textbook pages 38–40**

1. **Use counters, divide and fill in.**

   **a.** Divide 15 pencils equally between 3 children.
   How many pencils does each child get?

   $15 = 3 \times \boxed{\phantom{0}}$

   $15 \div 3 = \boxed{\phantom{0}}$ pencils

   Answer: Each child
   gets $\boxed{\phantom{0}}$ pencils.

   **b.** ★★★★★★★★★★★★

   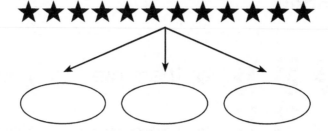

   Divide 12 ★ into 3 parts. Each part has $\boxed{\phantom{0}}$.

   Division sentence: $\boxed{\phantom{0}} \div \boxed{\phantom{0}} = \boxed{\phantom{0}}$

   **c.** Divide $\boxed{\phantom{0}}$ carrots equally between $\boxed{\phantom{0}}$ rabbits.
   How many carrots does each rabbit get?

   $\boxed{\phantom{0}} \div \boxed{\phantom{0}} = \boxed{\phantom{0}}$

   Answer: Each rabbit gets
   $\boxed{\phantom{0}}$ carrots.

**2.** Write the letter of the correct answer in the brackets.

   **a.** The quotient is 2, the divisor is 4 and the dividend is 8, so the correct sentence is (   ).

   **A.** 8 ÷ 2 = 4    **B.** 8 ÷ 4 = 2    **C.** 4 × 2 = 8    **D.** 2 × 4 = 8

   **b.** 30 ÷ 6 = 5    What does this sentence mean? (   )

   **A.** Divide 30 into 5 parts, and each part is 6.

   **B.** Divide 30 into 6 parts, and each part is 5.

**3.** Read each question carefully and work out the answer.

   **a.** A bag can hold 4 apples.
   How many bags can 12 apples be divided into?

   ☐ ÷ ☐ = ☐ bags        Answer: 12 apples can be divided into ☐ bags.

   **b.** Divide 12 apples into 3 parts. How many apples are there in each part?

   ☐ ÷ ☐ = ☐ apples        Answer: There are ☐ apples in each part.

_____ Level **B**

There are **20 oranges** and **48 bananas.**

   **a.** If each child is given 2 oranges, how many children can have oranges?

   **b.** 8 bananas fit into 1 box. How many boxes are needed for 48 bananas?

# 11. Using times tables to find the quotient

**Pupil Textbook page 41**

**1. Fill in the missing numbers.**

a. $5 \times \boxed{\phantom{0}} = 45$     $\boxed{\phantom{0}} \times 3 = 24$     $4 \times \boxed{\phantom{0}} = 36$

$40 = \boxed{\phantom{0}} \times 4$     $45 \div 5 = \boxed{\phantom{0}}$     $24 \div 3 = \boxed{\phantom{0}}$

$36 \div 4 = \boxed{\phantom{0}}$     $40 \div 4 = \boxed{\phantom{0}}$

b. $32 \div 8 = \boxed{\phantom{0}}$          $56 \div 7 = \boxed{\phantom{0}}$

We know ( ) eights          We know 7 (     )
are 32          are 56

so: $32 \div 8 = (\phantom{0})$          so: $56 \div 7 = (\phantom{0})$

**2. Write two multiplication sentences and two division sentences for each multiplication fact.**

| 4 times 7 is 28. | 2 times 9 is 18. | 5 times 8 is 40. |
|---|---|---|
| _____ | _____ | _____ |
| _____ | _____ | _____ |
| _____ | _____ | _____ |
| _____ | _____ | _____ |

**3. Work out the answers.**

$25 \div 5 =$     $60 \div 10 =$     $16 \div 4 =$     $18 \div 2 =$

$28 \div 4 =$     $35 \div 5 =$     $14 \div 2 =$     $24 \div 8 =$

**4.** Find all the suitable numbers.

☐ × 5 < 25

You could put these numbers in the ☐:

_____

☐ × 8 < 54

You could put these numbers in the ☐:

_____

**Follow the pattern to fill in the missing numbers.**

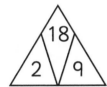 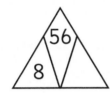 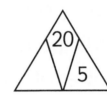 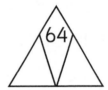

# 12. How many times?

**Pupil Textbook pages 42–44**　　　　　**Level A**

1. **Fill in the missing numbers, using the pictures to help you.**

   **a.**

If 4 oranges 🟠 are 1 part, watermelons 🍉 are ( ) parts. In other words the number of watermelons 🍉 is ( ) times the number of oranges 🟠.

☐ ÷ ☐ = ☐　　The number of watermelons 🍉 is ☐ times the number of oranges 🟠.

   **b.**

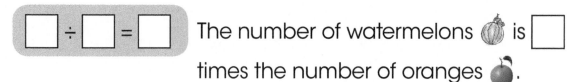

Apples: ☐

Strawberries: ☐

How many times greater is the number of apples than the number of strawberries?

☐ ÷ ☐ = ☐

The number of apples is ☐ times the number of strawberries.

## 2. Work out the answers.

**a.** How many times greater than 4 is 8?

**b.** What is 4 times 8?

**c.** How many is 4 times 4?

**d.** How many fours are there in 16?

## 3. Read each question carefully and work out the answer.

**a.** 32 fish must be divided equally between 4 fish bowls. How many fish go in each fish bowl?

**b.** There are 10 people in the small bus and 50 people in the big bus. How many times greater is the number of people in the big bus than the number of people in the small bus?

**1. There are 8 pens, 64 pencils and some crayons.**

    **a.** How many times greater is the number of pencils than the number of pens?

    **b.** The number of crayons is 3 times the number of pens. How many crayons are there?

    **c.** How many items are there altogether?

**2.** Ravi is 4 years old this year. His mother is 28 years old. His mother's age is (   ) times Ravi's age this year. Last year, his mother's age was (   ) times Ravi's age last year.

# 13. Division with the dividend 0

Level **A**

**1.** Calculate, using the pictures to help you.

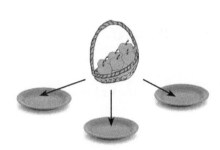

**a.** There are 6 apples in the basket. How many apples go on each plate to share the apples equally?

Division sentence:

_____

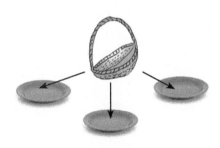

**b.** There are no apples in the basket. How many apples go on each plate to share the apples equally?

Division sentence:

_____

**2.** Mental calculation

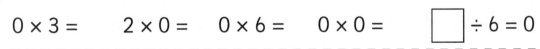

| | | | | |
|---|---|---|---|---|
| $0 \times 3 =$ | $2 \times 0 =$ | $0 \times 6 =$ | $0 \times 0 =$ | $\boxed{\phantom{0}} \div 6 = 0$ |
| $10 \times 0 =$ | $5 \times 0 =$ | $9 \times 0 =$ | $0 \times 100 =$ | $6 + \boxed{\phantom{0}} = 6$ |
| $0 \div 3 =$ | $0 \div 10 =$ | $0 \div 1 =$ | $0 + 0 =$ | $6 \div \boxed{\phantom{0}} = 6$ |
| $0 \div 100 =$ | $0 \div 2 =$ | $0 \div 9 =$ | $0 - 0 =$ | $\boxed{\phantom{0}} \div 2 = 6$ |

**3.** **Write the letter of the correct answer in the brackets.**

    **a.** The correct number sentence is (   ).

        **A.** $8 \times 0 = 8$    **B.** $8 \div 0 = 0$    **C.** $0 \div 8 = 0$    **D.** $8 - 0 = 0$

    **b.** One factor is 5 and the other factor is 0, so the product is (      ).

        **A.** $5 \times 0 = 5$    **B.** $0 \div 5 = 0$    **C.** $0 \times 5 = 0$    **D.** $0 + 5 = 5$

**4.** **Write the number sentences and calculate.**

    **a.** One factor is 7 and the other factor is 10. What is the product?

    **b.** The dividend is 0 and divisor is 10. What is the quotient?

    **c.** What is 4 times 5?

    **d.** How many times greater than 4 is 32?

    **e.** Divide 30 into 3 parts. How much is each part?

    **f.** How many tens are there in 30?

**1.** Think about the problem and work out the answers.

a. $\blacktriangle \times \blacktriangle = 25$

$\blacktriangle \times \blacksquare = 45$

$\blacksquare = ($ $)$

b. $\bullet \div \bigstar = 0$

$\bullet + \bigstar = 7$

$\bullet = ($ $) \bigstar = ($ $)$

**2.** Write the letter of the correct answer in the brackets.

$\bigstar + 42 = \blacktriangle + 24,$ $\bigstar ($ $) \blacktriangle$

**A.** $<$     **B.** $>$     **C.** $=$     **D.** cannot be compared to

# Unit Three: Statistics

Record the number of pupils competing in each event at sports day in a table.

The table below lists the sections in this unit.
After completing each section, assess your work.
(Use 😊 if you are satisfied with your progress or 😐 if you are not satisfied.)

| Section | Self-assessment |
|---|---|
| 1. Introduction to tables | |
| 2. Block diagrams | |

# 1. Introduction to tables

Pupil Textbook pages 51–53

**Dylan recorded all his classmates' favourite types of book.**

**a.** Complete the table using the data Dylan recorded.

| | |
|---|---|
| fairy tales | 卌 卌 |
| comic books | 卌 卌 卌 \| |
| reference books | \|\|\|\| |
| puzzle books | 卌 |

| Favourite type of book | Number of pupils |
|---|---|
| fairy tales | |
| comic books | |
| reference books | |
| puzzle books | |

**b.** Write the letter of the correct answer in the brackets.

The greatest number of pupils like reading (   ), and the smallest number like reading (   ).

**A.** fairy tales      **B.** comic books

**C.** reference books      **D.** puzzle books

**Look at the tables on the previous page. Think up some more questions and answer them.**

Question 1: _____

Number sentence: _____

Answer: _____

Question 2: _____

Number sentence: _____

Answer: _____

# 2. Block diagrams (1)

Pupil Textbook pages 54–59

Level **A**

**1.** Alex recorded the number of classmates who took part in each event on sports day.

   **a.** Complete the table using the data Alex recorded.

| skipping | ⊬⊬⊬ ⊬⊬⊬ |
|---|---|
| running | ⊬⊬⊬ ⊬⊬⊬ ⊬⊬⊬ I |
| throwing | II |
| jumping | ⊬⊬⊬ I |

| Event | skipping | running | throwing | jumping |
|---|---|---|---|---|
| Number of pupils | | | | |

**b.** Use the table to make a block diagram.

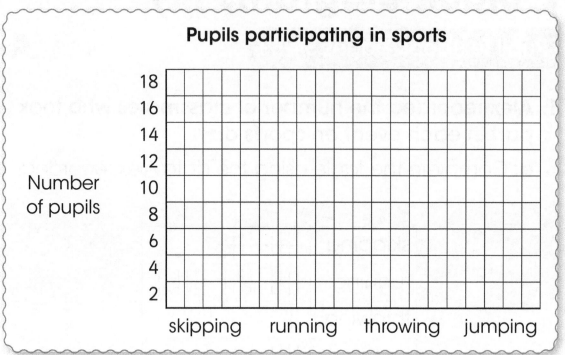

**Pupils participating in sports**

Number of pupils

18
16
14
12
10
8
6
4
2

skipping    running    throwing    jumping

**c.** Answer these questions based on the block diagram above.

**i.** How many more pupils did running than did skipping?
Number sentence: _____
Answer: _____

**ii.** How many times greater was the number of pupils doing jumping than those doing throwing?
Number sentence: _____
Answer: _____

**iii.** How many pupils participated in the sports day altogether?
Number sentence: _____
Answer: _____

**2. a.** Alex bought four kinds of snack for a class celebration. What snack did he buy most of? What snack did he buy least of?

| **3 bags of croissants** | **5 bags of bread rolls** | **2 bags of pastries** | **8 bags of cupcakes** |

 The number of croissants    ☐ × ☐ = ☐

 The number of bread rolls    ☐ × ☐ = ☐

 The number of pastries    ☐ × ☐ = ☐

 The number of cupcakes    ☐ × ☐ = ☐

Answer: The greatest number of snacks was (          ).
The smallest number of snacks was (          ).

**b.** Fill in the table of snacks.

| Snacks | Number |
|---|---|
| ![croissant] | |
| ![baguette] | |
| ![roll] | |
| ![cupcake] | |

**c.** Fill in the block diagram of snacks.

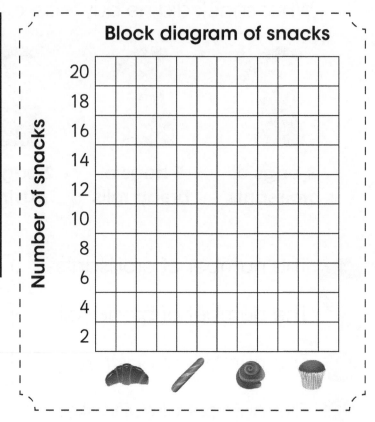

Level **B**

Think up some more questions based on the table and block diagram above and answer them.

Question 1:

_____

Number sentence:

_____

Question 2:

_____

Number sentence:

_____

# Unit Four: Multiplication and division (2)

Alex and 20 classmates are having an adventure in the park. There are 7 pupils in each group.

How many groups are there?

The table below lists the sections in this unit.

After completing each section, assess your work.

(Use 😊 if you are satisfied with your progress or 😐 if you are not satisfied.)

| Section | Self-assessment |
|---|---|
| 1. Multiplication and division of 7 | |
| 2. Multiplication and division of 3 | |
| 3. Multiplication and division of 6 | |
| 4. Multiplication and division of 9 | |
| 5. Relationships between multiplications of 3, 6 and 9 | |
| 6. Write multiplication and division questions | |
| 7. Splitting numbers into number sentences involving multiplication and addition | |
| 8. Division with remainders | |
| 9. Division calculations with remainders | |

53

# 1. Multiplication and division of 7

Pupil Textbook pages 61–63   Level **A**

1. **Find the rule and complete the sequence.**

    7, 14, 21, 28, ____, ____, ____, ____, ____, ____

2. **Mental calculations**

    | | | |
    |---|---|---|
    | $6 \times 7 + 13 =$ | $5 + 21 \div 7 =$ | $10 - 35 \div 7 =$ |
    | $28 + 8 \times 7 =$ | $10 \times 5 - 12 =$ | $42 - 9 \times 4 =$ |
    | $3 \times 8 + 8 =$ | $56 \div 7 - 7 =$ | |

3. **Write number sentences and work out the answers.**

    **a.** Divide 28 into 7 equal parts. How much is each part?

    **b.** What is 4 lots of 7?

    **c.** How many times greater is 35 than 7?

    **d.** What is 5 times 7?

**e.** How many sevens are there in 70?

**f.** The two factors are 7 and 10. What is the product?

Level **B**

Alex and 20 classmates are having an adventure in the park. There are 7 pupils in each group. How many groups are there?

# 2. Multiplication and division of 3

Pupil Textbook pages 64–65     Level A

**1.** Find the rule and complete the sequence.

3, 6, 9, 12, \_\_\_\_, \_\_\_\_, \_\_\_\_, \_\_\_\_, \_\_\_\_, \_\_\_\_

**2.** First complete the multiplication facts. Then write two multiplication number sentences and two division number sentences for each multiplication fact.

| | | |
|---|---|---|
| 3 sevens are ( ). | 3 (     ) are 27. | 3 (     ) are 24. |
| _____ | _____ | _____ |
| _____ | _____ | _____ |
| _____ | _____ | _____ |
| _____ | _____ | _____ |

**3.** Choose three numbers from 27, 7, 63, 3 and 9. Use your three numbers to write two multiplication number sentences and two division number sentences.

(   ) × (   ) = (   )     (   ) × (   ) = (   )

(   ) ÷ (   ) = (   )     (   ) ÷ (   ) = (   )

**4.** Read each question carefully and work out the answer.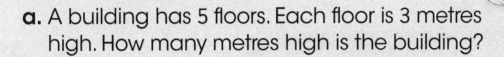

  **a.** A building has 5 floors. Each floor is 3 metres high. How many metres high is the building?

  **b.** There are 3 soft sweets and 18 hard sweets in a box. How many times as many hard sweets are there as soft sweets?

Level **B**

**1.** There are 4 seasons in a year and each one is 3 months long. How many months are there in a year?

**2.** Shortcut calculation

$3 + 6 + 9$

$= (\quad) \times 3$

$= (\quad)$

# 3. Multiplication and division of 6

**Pupil Textbook pages 66–67**

**Level A**

**1.** Choose three numbers from each group of numbers. Use your numbers to write two multiplication number sentences and two division number sentences.

| 6, 7, 8, 42 | 11, 5, 6, 30 | 2, 6, 12, 3 |
|---|---|---|
| _____ | _____ | _____ |
| _____ | _____ | _____ |
| _____ | _____ | _____ |
| _____ | _____ | _____ |

**2.** Write numbers in the brackets.

$$36 = \begin{cases} (\quad) \times (\quad) \\ (\quad) \times (\quad) \end{cases} \qquad 18 = \begin{cases} (\quad) \times (\quad) \\ (\quad) \times (\quad) \end{cases}$$

**3.** Which of the following numbers are products of multiplying by 6? Circle them.

24    12    18    6    28    60    30    45    70

**4. Mental calculations**

$9 + 6 \times 6 =$         $27 - 30 \div 6 =$         $45 - 5 \times 6 =$

$6 \div 6 + 6 =$         $24 \div 4 - 4 =$         $3 \times 6 - 2 =$

$0 \div 6 + 3 =$         $5 + 48 \div 6 =$

Level **B**

# What numbers do the shapes represent?

**a.** ☆ + ☆ + ☆ = 18

☐ + ☆ = 24

☆ = (     )      ☐ = (     )

**b.** ◯ + ◯ + △ + △ + △ = 24

◯ + ◯ + △ + △ + △ + △ + △ = 32

◯ = (     )      △ = (     )

# 4. Multiplication and division of 9

Pupil Textbook pages 68–69

Level **A**

**1. a.** Use the pictures to help you fill in the missing numbers.

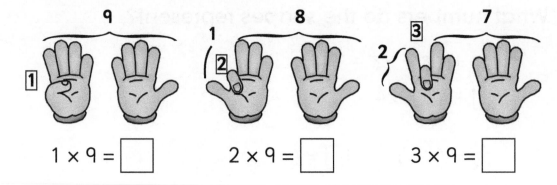

$1 \times 9 = \boxed{\phantom{0}}$      $2 \times 9 = \boxed{\phantom{0}}$      $3 \times 9 = \boxed{\phantom{0}}$

What did you find? Does the rest of the 9 times table make the same interesting pattern on your fingers? Try it out!

**b.** Complete the following number sentences. Use your fingers, as shown in the pictures above.

$4 \times 9 =$      $5 \times 9 =$      $6 \times 9 =$

$7 \times 9 =$      $8 \times 9 =$      $9 \times 9 =$

$18 \div 9 =$      $54 \div 9 =$      $63 \div 9 =$

$72 \div 9 =$      $81 \div 9 =$      $27 \div 9 =$

**2.** Find the rule and fill in the missing numbers.

1 × 9 = _____    How much less than 10? _____

2 × 9 = _____    How much less than 20? _____

3 × 9 = _____    How much less than 30? _____

6 × 9 = _____    _____ less than _____

7 × 9 = _____    _____ less than _____

9 × 9 = _____    _____ less than _____

**3.** There are 9 people per team. How many teams can be made with 45 people?

# 5. Relationships between multiplications of 3, 6 and 9

**Pupil Textbook page 70**

Level **A**

**1.** Complete the table.

| × | 1 | 2 | 3 | 4 | 5 | 6 | 7 | 8 | 9 | 10 |
|---|---|---|---|---|---|---|---|---|---|----|
| 3 |   |   |   |   |   |   |   |   |   |    |
| 6 |   |   |   |   |   |   |   |   |   |    |
| 9 |   |   |   |   |   |   |   |   |   |    |

**2. Fill in the missing numbers**

$1 \times 6 = \boxed{\phantom{0}} \times 3$     $2 \times 6 = \boxed{\phantom{0}} \times 3$     $4 \times 6 = \boxed{\phantom{0}} \times 3$

$2 \times 9 = \boxed{\phantom{0}} \times 3$     $2 \times 9 = \boxed{\phantom{0}} \times 6$     $3 \times 9 = \boxed{\phantom{0}} \times 3$

$30 = 3 \times \boxed{\phantom{0}} = \boxed{\phantom{0}} \times 6$          $36 = \boxed{\phantom{0}} \times 6 = 4 \times \boxed{\phantom{0}}$

**3. a.** A large pad of paper costs £6. How much do 2 large pads of paper cost?

 **b.** A small pad of paper costs £3. If you have £6, how many small pads of paper can you buy?

The door number of a person's house is a number less than 20.

The number is the product of number A and 6. It is also the product of number B and 9. What is the door number?

# 6. Write multiplication and division questions

**Pupil Textbook pages 72–73**

**Level A**

**Read each question carefully and work out the answer.**

**1. a.** There are 6 pupils in each group, and 5 groups in the class. How many pupils are there in the class?

**b.** The class has 30 pupils. They are divided into 5 groups. How many pupils are there in each group?

**c.** The class has 30 pupils, and there are 6 pupils in each group. How many groups are there?

**2.** Dylan's grandad keeps birds. He has 6 cages. There are 3 birds in each cage.

**a** How many birds does Dylan's grandad have?

**b** Dylan has 3 birds. How many times more birds than Dylan does his grandad have?

**c.** Dylan's grandad divides his birds equally between Alex and Poppy. How many birds does each of them get?

**d.** How many more birds should Dylan get so he has the same number as Poppy?

─────────────────────────────────────────

**1.** **Mrs Graham had £50. She bought 9 identical pens. She used £36 altogether. How much does each pen cost? How much money does Mrs Graham have left?**

**2. a.** Poppy bought 3 identical pens for £6. How much does each pen cost?

**b.** Dylan bought 6 of the same pens. How much did he spend?

**3.** Look at the picture and make up some mathematical questions. Write number sentences and give the answers.

**a.** There are 4 plates of apples. There are 3 applies on each plate.

Question:

_____

_____

Number sentence:

_____

Answer:

_____

_____

**b.** There are 12 apples altogether. There are 3 applies on each plate

Question:

_____

_____

Number sentence:

_____

Answer:

_____

_____

# 7. Calculations involving multiplication and addition

Level **A**

**1.** Look at the picture and write number sentences.

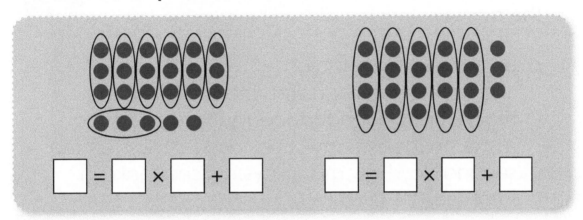

□ = □ × □ + □          □ = □ × □ + □

**2.** Fill in the missing numbers.

(Hint: Write the greatest possible number in each box.)

**a.**  12 = 1 × 10 + 2

12 = ☐ × 5 + (  )

12 = ☐ × 2

12 = ☐ × 4

12 = ☐ × 8 + (  )

12 = ☐ × 7 + (  )

12 = ☐ × 3

12 = ☐ × 6

12 = ☐ × 9 + (  )

**b.**  15 = 1 × 10 + (  )

15 = ☐ × 5

15 = ☐ × 2 + (  )

15 = ☐ × 4 + (  )

15 = ☐ × 8 + (  )

15 = ☐ × 7 + (  )

15 = ☐ × 3

15 = ☐ × 6 + (  )

15 = ☐ × 9 + (  )

**3.** **What is the greatest number that can go in the brackets?**

9 × (    ) < 64             8 × (    ) < 60

5 × (    ) < 36             6 × (    ) < 50

**4.** **Read each question carefully and work out the answer.**

  **a.** Lin works in a toy factory.
     She worked for 8 hours on the first day. If she
     made 5 toys per hour, how many toys did she
     make on the first day? She made 32 toys on the
     second day. How many toys did she make in
     total over the 2 days?

  **b.** There are 7 hens. There are 6 times this number
     of chicks. How many chicks are there? How
     many chicks and hens are there in total?

**1.** What numbers do the shapes represent?

△ ÷ □ = 3                     △ × □ = 27

△ = (     )                    □ = (     )

**2.** Try to write two different number sentences about the following picture.

(     ) × (     ) + (     ) = (     )

(     ) × (     ) − (     ) = (     )

# 8. Division with remainders

Level **A**

**1.** What is the greatest number that can go in the brackets?

2 × (    ) < 19      3 × (    ) < 26      (    ) × 4 < 29

**2.** Look at the pictures and write number sentences.

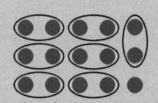

15 ÷ 2 = ☐ r ☐

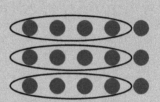

15 ÷ 4 = ☐ r ☐

**3.** Add circles first. Then write number sentences about the pictures.

**a.** Poppy has are 23 strawberries. Each plate holds 6 strawberries. How many plates can she fill? How many strawberries are left over?

☐ ÷ ☐ = ☐ plates r ☐ strawberries

Answer: Poppy can fill ☐ plates, with ☐ strawberries left over.

**b.** Emma has 14 apples to divide between boxes. Each box holds 5 apples. How many boxes can Emma fill. How many apples will be left over?

$\boxed{\phantom{0}} \div \boxed{\phantom{0}} = \boxed{\phantom{0}}$ boxes r $\boxed{\phantom{0}}$ apples

Answer: The apples can be divided between

$\boxed{\phantom{0}}$ boxes, with $\boxed{\phantom{0}}$ apples left over.

**1. Add circles first. Then write number sentences.**

**a.**

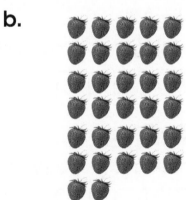

_____

**b.**

_____

**2. Fill in the missing numbers.**

**a.** ☆ $\div 4 = 9$ r $\boxed{\phantom{0}}$     What is the greatest remainder? (     )

**b.** △ $\div \boxed{\phantom{0}} = 2$ r 4     What is the smallest divisor? (     )

71

# 9. Division calculations with remainders

Level **A**

**1.** Use times tables to divide with remainders.

**a.** $17 \div 3 = 5$ r $2$

Thinking: 3 fives are $\boxed{15}$

$\boxed{17} - \boxed{15} = \boxed{2}$

**b.** $32 \div 9 =$

Thinking: ( ) nines are $\boxed{\phantom{0}}$

$\boxed{\phantom{0}} - \boxed{\phantom{0}} = \boxed{\phantom{0}}$

**c.** $40 \div 6 =$

Thinking: ( ) sixes are $\boxed{\phantom{0}}$

$\boxed{\phantom{0}} - \boxed{\phantom{0}} = \boxed{\phantom{0}}$

**d.** $18 \div 7 =$

Thinking: ( ) sevens are $\boxed{\phantom{0}}$

$\boxed{\phantom{0}} - \boxed{\phantom{0}} = \boxed{\phantom{0}}$

**2.** Mental calculations

| | | | |
|---|---|---|---|
| $19 \div 4 =$ | $21 \div 8 =$ | $43 \div 5 =$ | $59 \div 9 =$ |
| $25 \div 4 =$ | $47 \div 8 =$ | $31 \div 6 =$ | $31 \div 4 =$ |

**3.** Fill in the missing numbers.

**a.** ☐ ÷ 6 = 7 r 2

Thinking: 6 × 7 + 2 = ☐

**b.** ☐ ÷ 9 = 4 r 6

Thinking: 4 × 9 + 6 = ☐

**c.** ☐ ÷ 5 = 9 r 2

Thinking: 5 × 9 + 2 = ☐

**d.** ☐ ÷ 2 = 8 r 1

**e.** ☐ ÷ 10 = 3 r 4

**f.** ☐ ÷ 8 = 7 r 3

**4.** Read each question carefully and work out the answer.

**a.** 32 sweets are to be divided equally between 5 people. How many sweets will each person get? How many sweets will be left over?

**b.** There are 7 days in a week. In November there are 30 days. How many weeks are there in November and how many days are left over?

---

Level **B**

The following number sentence is a division with a remainder.

The greatest number the dividend can be is (   ).

☐ ÷ 6 = 5 r ☐

73

# Unit Five: Let's practise geometry

Find the rectangles, cuboids, squares and cubes in the picture.

The table below lists the sections in this unit.
After completing each section, assess your work.
(Use 😊 if you are satisfied with your progress or 😐 if you are not satisfied.)

| Section | Self-assessment |
|---|---|
| 1. Angles and right angles | |
| 2. Introduction to cubes and cuboids | |
| 3. Introduction to rectangles and squares | |

# 1. Angles and right angles

Level A

1. Which of these are angles? Write their numbers on the line.

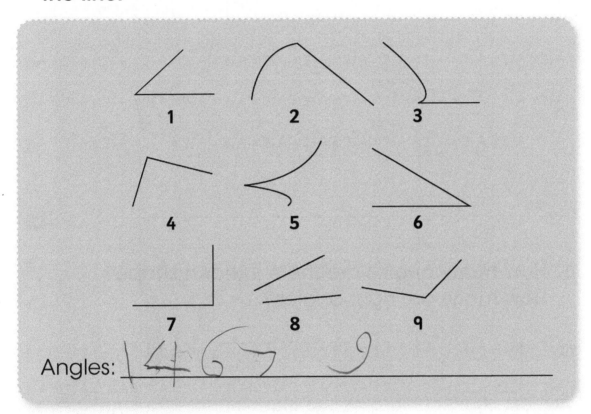

1    2    3

4    5    6

7    8    9

Angles: 1 4 6 7    9

2. Complete this.

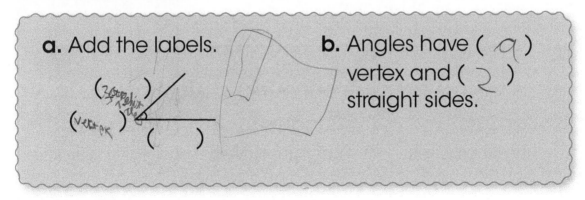

a. Add the labels.

( straight line )

( vertex )

( )

b. Angles have ( a ) vertex and ( 2 ) straight sides.

75

**3.** Use a set square to find right angles in the drawings below. Tick (✓) the right angles.

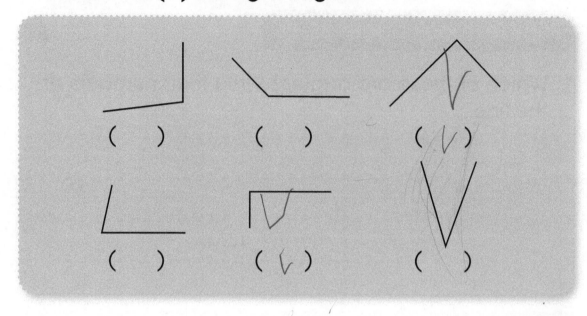

(    )          (    )          ( ✓ )

(    )          ( ✓ )          (    )

**1.** How many angles are there in each shape? How many are right angles?

a.

( 3 ) angles
( 1 ) right angles

b.

( 4 ) angles
( 4 ) right angles

c.

( 4 ) angles
( 4 ) right angles

d.

( 1 ) angles
( 1 ) right angles

e.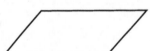

( 4 ) angles
( 0 ) right angles

f.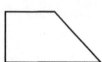

( 4 ) angles
( 2 ) right angles

**2.** Draw two angles on the grid. One must be a right angle.

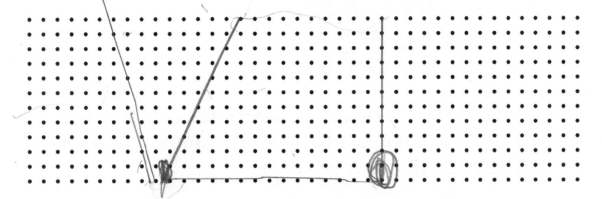

**3.** Dylan got home at 3 p.m. He said: 'The angle between the hour hand and the minute hand is a right angle.' Is he correct? Draw the hands on the clock and check.

Now try to find any other times where the angle between the hour hand and the minute hand is a right angle.

# 2. Introduction to cubes and cuboids

**Pupil Textbook pages 87–90**

**1.** Which of these shapes are cuboids? Which are cubes? Write their numbers on the lines. (Note that a cube is a cuboid too.)

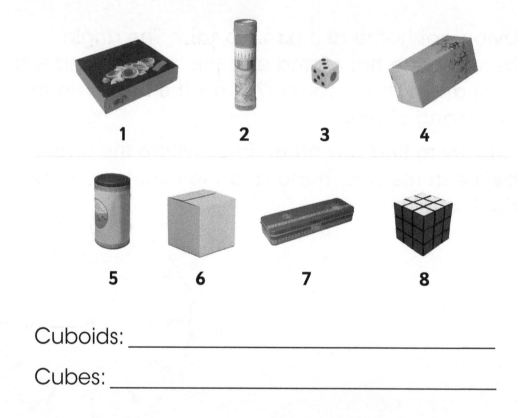

1          2          3          4

5          6          7          8

Cuboids: _____

Cubes: _____

**2.** Label each part of the cuboid and the cube.

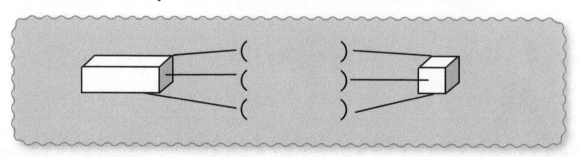

**3.** Fill in the missing numbers.

   **a.** A cube has (    ) vertices, (    ) edges and
   (    ) faces.

   **b.** A cuboid has (    ) vertices, (    ) edges and
   (    ) faces.

**4.** I am using small balls and sticks to make cube and
cuboid frames. How many more balls and sticks do
I need?

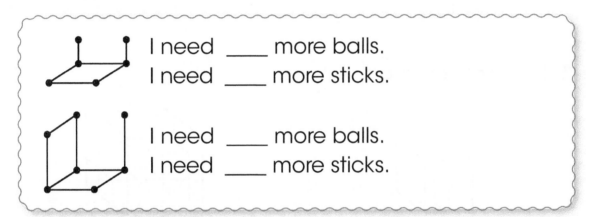

I need ____ more balls.
I need ____ more sticks.

I need ____ more balls.
I need ____ more sticks.

**5.** Let's count. How many cubes are needed to make
each of the shapes below?

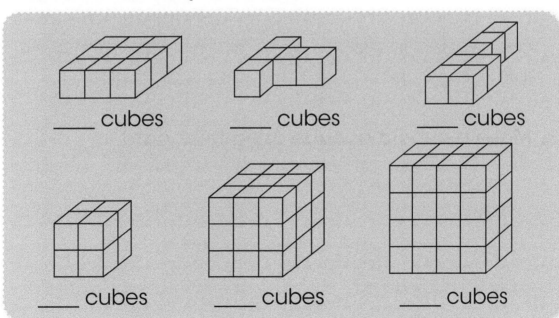

____ cubes          ____ cubes          ____ cubes

____ cubes          ____ cubes          ____ cubes

**1.** Let's count. How many cubes are needed to make each of the shapes below?

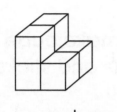 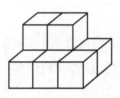 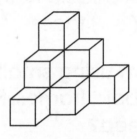

____ cubes    ____ cubes    ____ cubes

**2.** Fill in the missing numbers.

 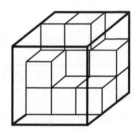

The shape has (    ) small cubes now. (    ) more small cubes are needed to make it into a big cube.

The shape has (    ) small cubes now. (    ) more small cubes are needed to make it into a big cube.

**3.** Make a cuboid or cube using thick card.

# 3. Introduction to rectangles and squares

Pupil Textbook pages 91–94     Level **A**

**1.** Which of the following shapes are rectangles? Which of them are squares? Write their numbers on the lines. (Note that a square is also a rectangle.)

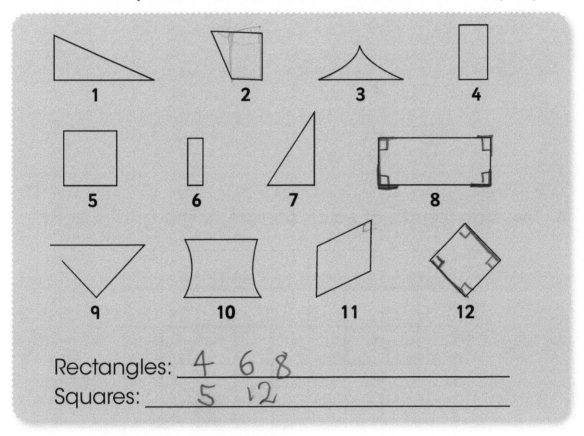

Rectangles: _4   6   8_
Squares: _5   ⅼ2_

**2. Complete the sentences.**

  **a.** A rectangle has ( 4 ) sides, and the opposite sides are ( parallel ). It has ( 4 ) angles and they are all ( right ) angles.

  **b.** A square has ( 4 ) sides, and they are ( same length ). It has ( 4 ) angles and they are all ( right ) angles.

3. **Draw these shapes on the centimetre-squared paper.**

   **a.** A square with a side length of 4 cm.
   **b.** A rectangle with side lengths of 5 cm and 3 cm.

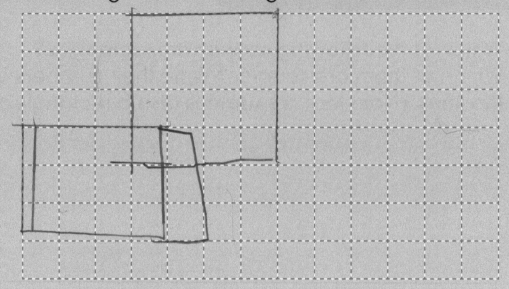

4. **The side length of each square of the grid is 1 cm.**

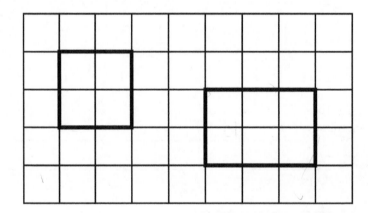

   **a.** The length of each side of the black square is
   2 cm.

   **b.** The side lengths of the black rectangle are 3 cm,
   2 cm, 3 cm and 2 cm.

## 5. Word problem

Dylan and Poppy made 8 squares in total with sticks. Dylan made 2 of the squares. How many squares did Poppy make? How many sticks did Dylan use?

Level **B**

## Count the shapes.

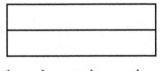

(   ) rectangles

(   ) squares

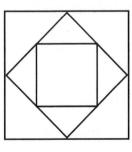

(   ) squares

# Unit Six: Consolidating and enhancing

The pupils go on an outing. 6 pupils sit in 1 boat. How many boats do 60 pupils need?

The table below lists the sections in this unit.
After completing each section, assess your work.
(Use 😊 if you are satisfied with your progress or 😐 if you are not satisfied.)

| Section | Self-assessment |
|---|---|
| 1. Let's multiply! | |
| 2. Multiplying and dividing games | |
| 3. 5 threes plus 3 threes equals 8 threes | |
| 4. 5 threes minus 3 threes equals 2 threes | |
| 5. Multiplication and division | |

# 1. Let's multiply!

Pupil Textbook page 96

Level **A**

## 1. Mental calculation

| | | | |
|---|---|---|---|
| 7 × 3 = | 2 × 4 = | 3 × 9 = | 2 × 9 = |
| 6 × 9 = | 4 × 8 = | 10 × 4 = | 8 × 7 = |
| 0 × 3 = | 5 × 3 = | 6 × 8 = | 8 × 5 = |
| 3 × 4 = | 7 × 7 = | 7 × 6 = | 5 × 6 = |

## 2. Fill in the missing numbers.

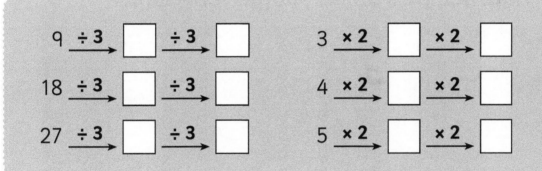

$$9 \xrightarrow{\div 3} \square \xrightarrow{\div 3} \square \qquad 3 \xrightarrow{\times 2} \square \xrightarrow{\times 2} \square$$

$$18 \xrightarrow{\div 3} \square \xrightarrow{\div 3} \square \qquad 4 \xrightarrow{\times 2} \square \xrightarrow{\times 2} \square$$

$$27 \xrightarrow{\div 3} \square \xrightarrow{\div 3} \square \qquad 5 \xrightarrow{\times 2} \square \xrightarrow{\times 2} \square$$

## 3. Write the maximum numbers possible in the brackets.

(   ) × 8 < 55          (   ) × 6 < 19          7 × (   ) < 30

23 > 9 × (   )          46 > 5 × (   )          60 > (   ) × 6

Level **B**

## 1. Write suitable numbers in the boxes.

4 = ☐ × ☐ | 9 = ☐ × ☐ | 16 = ☐ × ☐ | 25 = ☐ × ☐

36 = ☐ × ☐ | 49 = ☐ × ☐ | 64 = ☐ × ☐ | 81 = ☐ × ☐

12 = ☐ × ☐ = ☐ × ☐ | 24 = ☐ × ☐ = ☐ × ☐

## 2. What numbers do the shapes represent?

△ × ◯ = 18　　☐ × ◯ = 14　　☐ × △ = 63

△ = (　　)　　◯ = (　　)　　☐ = (　　)

# 2. Multiplying and dividing games

**Pupil Textbook page 97**

**Level A**

## 1. Mental calculation

$4 \times 5 =$          $8 \times 3 =$          $48 \div 6 =$

$35 \div 7 =$          $10 \times 6 =$          $18 \div 2 =$

$20 \div 4 =$          $49 \div 7 =$          $7 \times 9 =$

$7 \times 8 =$          $3 \times 10 =$          $36 \div 6 =$

$18 \div 9 + 10 =$          $32 - 9 \times 3 =$          $2 + 7 \times 4 =$

$70 - 30 \div 5 =$

## 2. Fill in the missing numbers.

| Factor | 3 | | 4 | 7 | |
|---|---|---|---|---|---|
| Factor | 6 | 5 | | | |
| Product | | 40 | 36 | 0 | 24 |

| Dividend | 8 | 32 | 9 | | |
|---|---|---|---|---|---|
| Divisor | 2 | | 9 | 5 | |
| Quotient | | 4 | | 10 | 8 |

**3.** Which oval should each card go in? Write each number sentence in the correct oval.

9 × 7

21 ÷ 3

6 × 9

10 × 5

4 × 8

30 ÷ 5

7 × 7

100 ÷ 1

32 ÷ 1

0 ÷ 100

64 ÷ 8

8 × 4

5 × 3

32 × 1

< 24

= 32

> 48

**4. Read each question carefully and work out the answer.**

a. There are 3 yellow flowers. The number of red flowers is 6 times the number of yellow flowers. How many red flowers are there?

b. The teacher has 48 balls and shares them equally between 8 bags. How many balls are in each bag?

c. A car can carry 5 people at the most. Can 8 cars carry 43 people?

d. Emma makes 6 small paper flowers. Dylan, Poppy and Alex each make the same number of small paper flowers as Emma. How many small paper flowers do Emma, Dylan, Poppy and Alex make in total?

**1.** Find the pattern and complete the sequence.

   **a.** 3, 6, 9, (    ), (    ), (    ), (    )

   **b.** 100, 81, 64, 49, 36, (    ), (    )

**2.** Complete the tables.

| × | 5 | 8 | 6 |
|---|---|---|---|
| 3 |   | 24 |   |
| 4 |   |   |   |

| × |   | 3 | 7 |
|---|---|---|---|
| 4 | 36 |   |   |
|   |   |   | 14 |

**3.**

There are 27 balloons.
What is the smallest number of balloons that can
be removed so that the rest of the balloons can
be shared equally between 5 children? How many
balloons does each child get?

# 3. 5 threes plus 3 threes equals 8 threes

Pupil Textbook page 98

Level **A**

**1. Look at the pictures and fill in the blanks.**

The total number of apples and pears is ____ groups of ____, plus ____ groups of ____, equals ____ groups of ____, which is _____.

$2 \times 3 + 4 \times 3 = \boxed{\phantom{0}} \times 3 = \boxed{\phantom{0}}$

**2. Complete the table. Then fill in the blank in the sentence.**

|          | 1  | 3  | 7 | 9 |
|----------|----|----|---|---|
| 2 times  | 2  |    |   |   |
| 5 times  | 5  | 15 |   |   |
| 7 times  | 7  |    |   |   |

2 times a number plus 5 times the same number is ____ times the number.

**3. Fill in the missing numbers.**

$3 \times 3 + 2 \times 3 = (\phantom{0}) \times 3$          $5 \times 3 + (\phantom{0}) \times 3 = 7 \times 3$

$3 \times 8 + 6 \times 8 = (\phantom{0}) \times 8$          $6 \times 5 + (\phantom{0}) \times 5 = 10 \times 5$

**4. Follow the examples to fill in the missing numbers.**

   **a.** $6 \times 4 + 2 \times 4 = 8 \times 4 = 32$

      $7 \times 3 + 2 \times 3 = (\ ) \times (\ ) = (\ )$

      $9 \times 3 + 9 \times 6 = (\ ) \times (\ ) = (\ )$

      $5 \times 7 + 7 \times 3 = (\ ) \times (\ ) = (\ )$

   **b.** $9 \times 7 = 8 \times 7 + 1 \times 7$

      $9 \times 7 = 7 \times 7 + 2 \times 7$

      $9 \times 7 = (\ ) \times 7 + (\ ) \times 7$

      $9 \times 7 = 9 \times (\ ) + 9 \times (\ )$

**5. Read each question carefully and work out the answer.**

   **a.** There are 10 black fish and 30 red fish in the fish tank. The number of red fish is how many times the number of black fish?

   **b.** The school has 47 footballs, which are divided equally between 9 classes. How many footballs does each class get? How many footballs are left over?

**1.** Think about the times table first. Then fill in the missing numbers.

  **a.** $11 \times 6 = 1 \times 6 + 10 \times 6$

  $11 \times 6 = ($     $) \times ($     $) + ($     $) \times ($     $)$

  $11 \times 6 = ($     $) \times ($     $) + ($     $) \times ($     $)$

  $11 \times 6 = ($     $) \times ($     $) + ($     $) \times ($     $)$

  $11 \times 6 = ($     $) \times ($     $) + ($     $) \times ($     $)$

  **b.** $7 \times 9 + 7 = 7 \times \boxed{\phantom{0}}$

  **c.** $2 \times 6 + 3 \times 6 + 4 \times 6 = \boxed{\phantom{0}} \times \boxed{\phantom{0}}$

**2.** There are **6** pens in a box. Alex buys **2** boxes of pens. Poppy buys **3** boxes of pens. How many pens do they buy altogether?

# 4.5 threes minus 3 threes equals 2 threes

**Pupil Textbook page 99**  Pupil Textbook page 99  Level **A**

**1. Look at the pictures and fill in the blanks.**

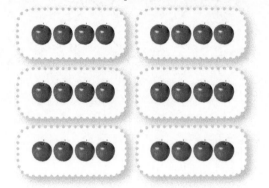 

How many more apples than pears?

You can work it out like this:

____ groups of ____ minus ____ groups of ____ equals ____ groups of ____, which is _____.

$6 \times 4 - 4 \times 4 = \boxed{\phantom{0}} \times 4 = \boxed{\phantom{0}}$

**2. Complete the table. Then fill in the blank in the sentence.**

|         | 1 | 4  | 6 | 8 |
|---------|---|----|---|---|
| 9 times | 9 | 36 |   |   |
| 6 times | 6 |    |   |   |
| 3 times |   |    |   |   |

9 times a number minus 6 times the same number is ____ times the number.

**3. Fill in the missing numbers.**

$7 \times 3 - 4 \times 3 = (\phantom{0}) \times 3$    $7 \times 5 - (\phantom{0}) \times 5 = 5 \times 5$

$9 \times 5 - 3 \times 5 = (\phantom{0}) \times 5$    $12 \times 7 - (\phantom{0}) \times 7 = 6 \times 7$

**4.** Follow the examples to fill in the missing numbers.

   **a.** $8 \times 4 - 6 \times 4 = 2 \times 4 = 8$
   $9 \times 3 - 5 \times 3 = (\quad) \times (\quad) = (\quad)$
   $8 \times 8 - 8 \times 4 = (\quad) \times (\quad) = (\quad)$
   $5 \times 7 - 7 \times 3 = (\quad) \times (\quad) = (\quad)$

   **b.** $5 \times 7 = 6 \times 7 - 1 \times 7$
   $5 \times 7 = 7 \times 7 - 2 \times 7$
   $5 \times 7 = (\quad) \times 7 - (\quad) \times 7$
   $5 \times 7 = 5 \times (\quad) - 5 \times (\quad)$

**5.** Write >, = or < in each ◯.

$54 \div 9 \bigcirc 6$       $8 \times 3 \bigcirc 24$       $3 \bigcirc 27 \div 3$

$45 \div 9 \bigcirc 40 \div 10$       $7 + 36 \bigcirc 36 - 7$       $10 \div 10 \bigcirc 5 \div 5$

**6.** Read each question carefully and work out the answer.

   **a.** The pupils are at the boating lake.
   Each boat can take 6 pupils. How many boats
   are needed for 60 pupils?

**b.** Alex takes some money from his money box. He spends 48p on 6 identical pencils and gets 2p change. How much did Alex take out of his money box? How much did he pay for each pencil?

**1.** Think about the problems first. Then fill in the missing numbers.

$12 \times 4 - 7 \times 4 = 5 \times 4 = 20$

$13 \times 8 - 3 \times 8 = (\quad) \times (\quad) = (\quad)$

$6 \times 15 - 6 \times 10 = (\quad) \times (\quad) = (\quad)$

$11 \times 5 - 5 \times 7 = (\quad) \times (\quad) = (\quad)$

$11 \times 9 - 9 = (\quad) \times (\quad) = (\quad)$

**2.** There are 6 pens in a box. Alex buys 8 boxes of pens. Poppy buys 5 boxes of pens. How many more pens does Alex buy than Poppy?

# 5. Multiplication and division

Level **A**

**1. Write each number sentence and calculate.**

  **a.** Two factors are 7. What is their product?

  **b.** The dividend is 40. The divisor is 5. What is the quotient?

  **c.** 36 is divided into 6 equal parts. How much is each part?

  **d.** How many nines are there in 45?

**e.** How many times greater than 6 is 54?

**f.** What is 8 times 7?

**g.** What is the total when you add 3 sixes?

**h.** What is the product of multiplying 8 by 2?

**2.** Read each question carefully and work out the answer.

a. There are 5 white rabbits. The number of grey rabbits is 4 times the number of white rabbits. How many grey rabbits are there?

b. There are 12 pens and 6 pencils. The number of pens is how many times the number of pencils?

c. 25 apples are shared equally between 6 plates. How many apples are there on each plate? How many apples are left over?

**d.** The fruit shop sells lots of pears and apples.
Mr Shelley packs boxes of 9 pears or 6 apples.

   **i.** He packs a total of 7 boxes of pears. How many
      pears are there?

   **ii.** There is a total of 60 apples. How many boxes
       can he pack?

   **iii.** How many fewer apples are there than pears?

1. The pupils go boating. Each boat can take 6 people. There are 18 girls. The boys fit in exactly 2 boats. Is the number of girls greater or less than the number of boys? (Try to compare them using different methods.)

   Method 1:                    Method 2:

2. Think about the problem and then work out the answer.

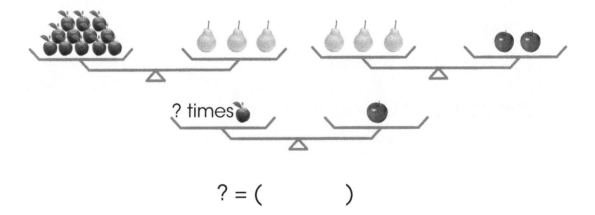

   ? times

   ? = (          )

### 3. Maths game: Grab a number!

The rules of the game are:

- Pupils A and B play together.
- First choose a number that is greater than 2 as the Grab Number.
- Then, starting from 1, count: 1, 2, 3 ...
- Each pupil can count either one or two numbers.
- The pupil who first reaches the Grab Number wins.

For example, the Grab Number chosen is **9**.

    A: 1
    B: 2, 3
    A: 4, 5
    B: 6
    A: 7
    B: 8, 9     **B wins!**

Can you win? Go on, try the game!